What Hat Are You Wearing?

Story by
Marion Green, LMFT and Liz Barron
Illustrated by Erin Williams

LUMINARE PRESS
WWW.LUMINAREPRESS.COM

What Hat Are You Wearing?

Printed in the United States of America

Illustrated by Erin Williams

Luminare Press
442 Charnelton St.
Eugene, OR 97401
www.luminarepress.com

LCCN: 2022902838
ISBN: 978-1-64388-939-9

*For kids of all ages
who want to choose to feel their best
in everyday situations—both big and small.*

Once there was a cool kid named Nina.
She was strong, brave, and happy.
Nina loved how great her life could be...
most of the time.

Nina spent a lot of time being
happy with her parents,

playful with her brother,

and silly with her friends...
all feelings that she really liked.

But for some reason, Nina also had feelings that made her feel unhappy sometimes.

When her mom asked her to get ready for bed, even though she knew it was safe, she would imagine scary things.

When her friend Jay said that
he was excited about going
on vacation with his family,

all Nina could think about was how nervous he might feel being around so many strangers. Nina knew that she was spending too much time worrying, but she just didn't know how to make herself feel better.

One day, Nina's favorite babysitter,
Mrs. Whiskers, came over to take care of her.

Nina loved talking to Mrs. Whiskers because she always had a way of making her feel better. When Nina shared that she had been feeling worried lately, Mrs. Whiskers suggested that they take a trip down to her favorite store, Cool Cat Hats!

When they walked inside, Nina was amazed by all of the different kinds of hats!

There were winter hats to keep you warm, baseball hats to block the sun, and even funny hats for playing dress up.

"Did you know that your feelings are like hats?" asked Mrs. Whiskers. "Just like you can choose a hat... you can choose a feeling!"

Mrs. Whiskers could tell Nina was curious and asked her if she wanted to make her very own cool cat hat. Nina was thrilled! "The hat you are going to make will have magic. It will help you see that you can change feelings you don't want into feelings you do want!" exclaimed Mrs. Whiskers.

Nina looked puzzled. "What do you mean?" she asked. "Your new hat will remind you that you always have the power to choose how you want to feel about what's happening," explained Mrs. Whiskers.

Nina thought for a bit and said, "So do you mean that at bedtime, I can imagine wearing my cool cat hat and feeling brave instead of being scared?" "Yes exactly!" said Mrs. Whiskers. "Just thinking about your special hat will help you remember that you can pick the feelings you want to have!"

Nina went right to work making her special hat. She cut her favorite color ribbon, picked out pretty flowers, and even chose little lady bugs as decorations.

When Nina was done, Mrs. Whiskers helped her glue everything on and make the final touches.

Mrs. Whiskers admired Nina's creation and said, "Wow this is fantastic!" Nina glowed with pride and she could feel the hat's magic waking up her new superpower. "Now don't forget to imagine your special hat anytime you want to change your feelings Nina," said Mrs. Whiskers.

"All you have to do is ask yourself, 'How do I want to feel right now?' Your superpower will start to work and you will begin to feel the way that you want."

"So Nina," Mrs. Whiskers continued, "your special hat can change from a shy-hat to a confident-hat or a frustrated-hat to a patient-hat...the possibilities are endless! And the best part is that you get to choose what feeling you want to have."

On their way home, Nina said that she didn't want to walk anymore and that she didn't like the noise from the cars zooming by.

"Nina, what hat are you wearing?" asked Mrs. Whiskers. Nina stopped in her tracks and replied, "I guess I'm wearing a grumpy-hat."

"Well you have the power to change that, what feeling-hat would you like to wear instead?" asked Mrs. Whiskers. Nina paused, "a good mood-hat!"

COOL CATS hats

Suddenly, Nina began to notice the sun shining and the prettiness all around her and she instantly felt better. "Hey!" she exclaimed, "I really can change my feelings! The power is within me, just like a cool cat kid!"

Nina began to think about all of the things that she had spent so much time worrying about. "Do I want to feel shy about meeting new friends or afraid of trying new activities?" she asked herself. "Nope!" she decided, and imagined wearing an excited-hat which made her feel better instead.

When Nina got home, she proudly showed her cool cat hat to her family. She told them how she could now change her unhappy feelings into feelings she liked better.

They were so excited to know that Nina could use her new superpower to turn her kitty frown upside down.

Marion Green is a Licensed Marriage and Family Therapist who has been practicing in CT for over 20 years. She treats clients of all ages and especially enjoys working with children and their families. She and her husband, Jim, have been married for 30+ years and have two grown daughters.

Liz Barron is a freelance writer and staff writer for Moffly Media publications who lives in CT. Prior to her career in writing, she worked at an NYC-based investment bank. She and her husband, Mike, have two young children and a German Shepherd named Fenway.

Erin Williams is a self-taught artist who specializes in children's book illustrations, editorial work, and print design. She lives in CO with her husband and three young kids.

Made in United States
North Haven, CT
08 September 2022

23825134R20020